Introdu

Why read this book?

This book is for any teacher who's interested in improving their practice.

It outlines a set of mindsets and habits you can use to help you identify the most impactful parts of your teaching, and put them center stage.

It's about doing less to achieve more.

But it's also about being happier and more confident in the classroom. Building stronger routines around the essentials will give you more time and space to appreciate and think creatively about your work.

Lean Lesson Planning:
a practical approach to doing less
and achieving more in the classroom.

Copyright © 2019 Peps Mccrea
Version 4.2, October 2019

Published by **John Catt**
ISBN 978 1 912906 68 0

*To Mum, Dad and all you other
legends out there.*

Roadmap

About Peps

Peps Mccrea is an award-winning teacher educator, designer and author.

He is Dean of Learning Design at Ambition Institute, author of the High Impact Teaching series, and holds fellowships from the Young Academy and University of Brighton.

Peps has three Masters degrees, two lovely kids, and dances like no-one is watching (which is probably for the best).

Visit **pepsmccrea.com** for the full shebang.

Primer

Make the most of this book.

This book is a result of the lessons I've learned as a teacher and teacher educator, of my experiences helping hundreds of teachers to raise their game.

Where possible, I've tried to ground my work in the most compelling evidence about what works in the classroom.

I draw heavily on thinking from heavyweights like Hattie, Wiliam and Lemov[1]. Many of the ideas in this book are not new. They've just been re-framed with a focus on lesson planning.

This book is not a theoretical think piece, nor a practical blueprint. It is a set of tools and strategies you can use as a starting point for **experimentation in context**.

It doesn't contain specific examples, which can sometimes narrow down practice prematurely. Instead, it uses 'ask yourself' questions to help you identify improvements in practice that will work in your situation.

As with any self-improvement activity, you get what you put in. Without action, there will be no change.

Taking the time to answer these questions properly is an essential step towards *doing less and achieving more*. There are no quick fixes. If you're looking for ways to short-cut the amount of time you spend lesson planning, then this book is not for you.

Finding your way around.

Lean lesson planning is composed of three acts.

ACT I sets the scene, offering an overview of the meanings, mindsets and habits underpinning the lean approach. **ACT II** unpicks the core habits of lean planning in detail, and then **ACT III** takes a step back and outlines a set of strategies for managing our own individual and collective improvement.

Where relevant, each chapter ends with some notes and suggestions for further reading.

I've tried to keep my writing as concise as possible, so you can spend less time reading, and more time putting ideas into practice.

Now open your mind and drink it all in.

Notes & further reading

1. If you're serious about improving, I'd highly recommend you get your hands on the following three books:
- *Visible Learning for Teachers* by John Hattie
- *Practice Perfect* by Doug Lemov
- *Embedded Formative Assessment* by Dylan Wiliam

ACT I

Lean foundations

1

Defining lean

"It is not that we have a short time to live, but that we waste a lot of it."
- Seneca[1]

When society has a problem, it often turns to education for a fix. Recently, society has experienced some major upheaval. Teachers are subject to more pressure and higher expectations than ever before.

And yet, the greatest challenge we face is not one that society generates for us. It is one that comes from within.

It is the battle with ourselves. In particular, how best to spend our time. Where to focus our energy and attention, and how to ensure our actions line up with our intentions.

This challenge is not a new one. But changes in the landscape are making it ever more complex to navigate. It is no surprise that in some areas, 50% of the profession leave within their first five years[2.]

I believe that one of the biggest professional challenges of our time is to help teachers make better use of their time.

As part of this we need to start asking whether traditional models of planning are still fit for purpose. **I'm excited to kickstart a rethink.**

The meaning of lean.

The concept of lean is not new. It has its roots in the manufacturing industry, and more recently has found its feet in software development.

Lean is about optimizing productivity, about maximizing impact for every unit of input. It achieves this by raising the status of high-impact activities, eliminating waste, and making continual, incremental improvements over time.

In the context of the classroom, lean is about achieving as much learning as possible from every minute spent planning and teaching.

It's about directing your attention towards the things that matter, and making small changes to your everyday routines that add up to big gains over time. It's about doing less to achieve more.

> *"The best place to look is for small changes in the things we do most often."*
> - Henry Eyring

Notes & further reading

1. From *On the Shortness of Life*
2. For more, see *The birth of a zombie statistic* by Sam Freedman goo.gl/w7eLIV

2

Lean mindsets

Mindsets are powerful things[1]. They are lenses through which we make sense of ourselves and the world, and our capacity to change both.

Trying to use the right tactics with the wrong mindsets is like swimming against the current. You'll make slow, exhausting progress, and end up back where you started.

That's why I'm advocating a *mindsets-first approach*. The following four **lean mindsets** offer a robust platform upon which you can build the rest of your lean planning approach.

If you already use these mindsets, they will seem fairly obvious. If you don't, they might feel a little uncomfortable at first.

Either way, there's value in knowing your options, and being intentional about your choices.

'Process' mindset.

Unlean mindset	Lean mindset
Planning as a filled-in form	Planning as a thinking process

Planning is best viewed as a process rather than a product. As a stack of **habits of thought** that you bring into play to prepare yourself for teaching.

It is not a fixed set of procedures that you have to follow, nor a beautifully filled in form.

Sometimes we confuse the plan with the planning, as if they are the same thing. This can lead to situations where planning becomes an exercise in *form filling* rather than *hard thinking*.

That is not to say that having a plan is unimportant. Documentation has its uses, and is required in certain situations. However, it's best treated as a by-product and little more.

> *"Plans are worthless, but planning is everything."*
> \- Dwight Eisenhower

'Pareto' mindset.

The Pareto Principle (or 80/20 rule) suggests that in many areas of life, 80% of the impact comes from 20% of the inputs. Planning and teaching is no exception.

Unlean mindset	Lean mindset
Do as much as possible	Do less but do it better

This means that the bulk of your impact is due to a small fraction of the things you do and think about during planning. It means that some parts of the process are more productive than others.

The impact of your effort is not evenly distributed.

Lean lesson planning is about identifying those parts of your planning which deliver the greatest results, the tools and habits that make the most difference, and focusing on them ruthlessly[3.]

It's about doing less but doing it better.

> "The most important thing I've learned about planning is that it needs to be efficient. So I've tried to isolate the parts of planning that have the biggest impact on my teaching, and I make sure to do those (pretty much) every day."
> - Michael Pershan[3]

'Growth' mindset.

If you're familiar with Carol Dweck's work[4], then this will be old news. Lesson planning is a process that is learned, not a skill that is inherited. Great lesson planners are made, not born.

Unlean mindset	Lean mindset
Some people are naturally better at planning	Anyone can become a great planner with the right practice

That is not to say that some people aren't better than others. Just that you've got control over how good you can be. About how regularly you reflect on your planning, and how much effort you put into making it better.

The way you plan is heavily influenced by how those around you do it. School life is busy and changes come so relentlessly that your planning can easily end up being shaped by your local situation, rather than deliberate choices about what is important.

'Design' mindset.

Imagine you are building a bridge, and you want to make some radical changes. Would you talk to your builder, or would you talk to your architect?

Being sensible, you'd talk to both of course. However, all being equal, time spent with your architect will lead to more fundamental and wide-reaching changes.

It's the same for building learning. Changes in planning will generally lead to more substantial improvements than tweaking your performance.

Unlean mindset	Lean mindset
I get better by trying stuff out in the classroom	I improve by making systematic changes in my planning

One reason for this is that the classroom is a *hot environment*. It's a place where teachers have to make hundreds, if not thousands of decisions each lesson. The vast majority of these are automatic, intuitive responses that are executed with minimal deliberation.

Planning, however, happens mostly in a *cold environment*, where you have time to weigh your options, anticipate their outcomes, and arrive at a considered decision[5]. Planning allows us to make more **intentional changes to our practice**. In short, planning makes possible.

> *"By failing to plan, you are planning to fail."*
> - Alan Lakein

Before you read on, revisit the four lean mindsets. Ask yourself: **Which mindsets do I most frequently adopt? Which ones do my colleagues use?**

Notes & further reading

1. For a good introduction, read *Mindset* by Carol Dweck
2. For more, see 'Practise the 20' in *Practice Perfect* by Doug Lemov, p.29
3. From *How I plan: the triage* goo.gl/3E6bP1
4. See note 1 above
5. For more, read *Thinking, Fast and Slow* by Daniel Kahneman

	Unlean Mindset	Lean Mindset
Process	Planning as a filled-in form	Planning as a thinking process
Parento	Do as much as possible	Do less but do it better
Growth	Some people are naturally better at planning	Anyone can become a great planner with the right practice
Design	I get better by trying stuff out in the classroom	I improve by making systematic changes in my planning

Fig. 1   The 4 lean mindsets

3

Lean habits

Planning, like architecture, is an exercise in design. A stormy marriage of process and creativity. Where science and art collide.

Designers use tried-and-tested, step-by-step approaches alongside bursts of divergent thinking to achieve their goals.

The challenge for the lean lesson planner is to figure out which parts of the planning process are best followed *consistently*, and which parts are best tackled *creatively*.

Which parts should stay the same, and which parts should change.

An overarching 'lean framework'.

You will inevitably find your own balance between consistency and creativity, but, there are some elements of the process which I'd recommend keeping the same in the majority of cases.

These non-variables build upon the foundations laid by the lean mindsets, and provide a narrative framework around which you can hang your planning routine.

They may seem like a very obvious set of questions. Ironically, it is this obviousness that makes them all-too-often overlooked.

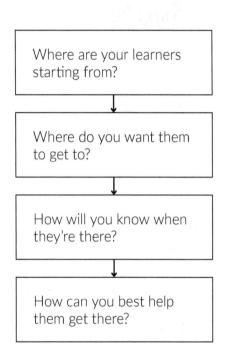

Fig. 2   The lean framework

Many teachers jump straight into the detail of planning before considering their broader strategy. They get sucked into the ineffective habit of starting their planning with the final question in the framework.

In my experience, taking shortcuts through the lean framework can be costly. Leave a question out or get them in the wrong order and you immediately limit the potential impact of your planning.

"Give me six hours to chop down a tree and I will spend the first four sharpening the axe."
- Abraham Lincoln

Take a moment to ask yourself: **What questions do I ask myself when I plan? How consistent and intentional is my strategy?**

Introducing the lean habits.

Whilst the lean framework provides a solid scaffold for your planning, it doesn't offer enough detail to help you build effective practice. For this, we need to dive into the *essential habits of planning*.

Remember that these are not a blueprint, but a set of tools to use as a starting point for disciplined self-improvement.

The remainder of this book dedicates a chapter to each of these habits. The first six focus on ways to improve your planning. The final three explore ways to organize your own professional learning.

Before you move on, take a moment to reflect on the ideas we've explored so far, on the meaning, mindsets and framework of *lean*. Ask yourself: **How lean is my practice? What steps can I take right now to do less and achieve more?**

Think about what you've learned and ready yourself for more. It's time to dig into the habits of lean planning. Prepare for ACT II.

Planning

Backwards design Start with the end in mind.

Knowing Knowledge Establish your route towards expertise.

Checking Understanding Build on what they know, not what they don't.

Efficient activities Select and streamline for the shortest path.

Lasting learning Build memory that lasts and is easy to recall.

Inter-lesson planning Plan for the past and into the future.

Growing

Building excellence Leverage habits to create lasting change.

Growth teaching Innovate, evaluate and iterate to improve.

Collective improvement Get better together for compound growth.

Fig. 3   The 9 lean habits

ACT II

Habits for planning

4

Backwards design

"If you don't know where you're going, you'll probably end up someplace else."
- Laurence Peter

I have worked with many teachers who have become frustrated by the planning habits they've developed over time. In some cases, this is because they have fallen unexpectedly into one or both of the following classic traps[1].

1. **Activity-focused planning** starts by trying to find a good activity, and then reverse engineering the lesson intentions to match the likely outcomes of the activity. Over time, this approach can end up becoming an exercise in *keeping students busy*.
2. **Coverage-focused planning** begins with a set of lesson intentions that have been crafted by someone else (eg. a colleague or a textbook), rather than taking the time to construct aims around your student needs. Over time, teaching can become an exercise in *getting through the curriculum*.

It *is* possible to experience some short-term gains with both of these approaches. They offer easy and compelling solutions to the problem of planning.

However, they are economically flawed, and over time, are likely to stifle professional creativity and generate poor levels of return on student learning.

Starting with the end in mind.

In his recent mega-meta analysis[2], John Hattie argues that one of the best ways to optimize learning is to use backwards design. In the context of lean lesson planning this means two things.

1. Starting your planning with the question:
   What do I want my students to have learnt by the end of the lesson?
2. Spending more time on this activity than you think you should.

Doug Lemov observed that effective teachers spend more time *identifying outcomes* and less time *selecting activities* than their colleagues[3].

The clearer you are about where you want to go, the better chance you have of getting there.

This logic may seem obvious, but in practice, it is frequently prone to abuse.

Backwards design is about striving for **excessive clarity** about what you want your students to be able to do as they progress through the lesson.

This involves mapping out, breaking down and thinking hard about how the various parts of the learning trajectory hang together.

One of the easiest ways to do this is to identify a range of **learning milestones** for your lesson. Tasks that your students are unable to do at the start of the lesson, but with support, may achieve by the end.

It's best to aim for between two to five milestones. Any more and you'll begin to dilute their resolution.

Get these right and the rest of your planning will be easier and more effective. You'll also have a powerful set of touchstones that we'll be coming back to in many of the habits that follow.

Effective learning milestones.

The way you craft your learning milestones will influence how useful they are. Effective milestones are:

- **Cumulative** They build on one another, so just like milestones in real life, passing one will take you closer to the next.

- **Distributed** They are spread out in such a way that the majority of students can pass the first, but few can pass the last.

- **Measurable** They are clearly signposted so you can easily tell when your students have passed them.

- **Clear** They are phrased in such a way that you and your students can quickly understand what they aiming for.

The better your students understand their learning milestones, the more directly they can make progress towards them.

This entails more than just asking them to copy the milestones from the board. It involves taking time to help them understand what they mean, and ideally, showing what passing them looks like[4.]

Backwards design is a simple idea, but it's not always easy to put into practice. Changing habits of thought takes time and repeated effort. But if you're genuinely interested in leveraging your impact, it's an investment highly worth making.

Notes & further reading

1. For more on backwards design and the 'twin-sins' of planning, read *Understanding by Design* by Wiggins & McTighe goo.gl/O3mlyY
2. *Visible Learning* by John Hattie
3. From *Practice Perfect* by Doug Lemov
4. For more, read *Embedding Formative Assessment* by Dylan Wiliam

5

Knowing knowledge

In the mid-nineties Stigler and Hiebert conducted a mammoth study comparing teaching between different countries[1.]

The practice they observed varied more than expected. The approaches of some countries had substantially greater impact than others.

One of the most significant factors was how teachers balanced their time between *teaching for conceptual understanding* and *teaching for technical proficiency.*

In their study, teachers in the US placed more emphasis on building technical proficiency, at the expense of conceptual understanding. Japanese teachers opted for a more balanced approach and achieved better results.

The message here is not that we should be striving for some perfect knowledge-time formula, but that our impact on learning is limited by our *understanding* of the different dimensions of knowledge, and how they hang together.

Lean lesson planning is about being sensitive to those nuances. It's about making deliberate choices about what to focus on and when, and selecting activities to match your goals.

It's about knowing knowledge, and how to build it.

A tool analogy for knowledge.

In my experience, one of the most helpful ways to think about knowledge is as a set of mental tools that we construct and master over time[2].

In this analogy, the act of building tools in our head is equivalent to **conceptual understanding**, and the act of mastering them is equivalent to **technical proficiency**[3].

Imagine you are learning about the area of a circle. The tool you are trying to construct is a mental model or map of that idea.

You can construct a very basic version of that tool by memorizing the formula, or a more sophisticated version by making sense of what the area of a circle means, why the formula works, and how the different components relate to each other.

The power of conceptual understanding is a product of how well **connected** it is. An isolated fact grows in power as you link it to other facts, eventually becoming part of a dense network of meaning that intertwines with, and augments what you already know[4.]

The more connected a fact becomes, the more it *makes sense*.

Being able to answer questions hung around certain verbs can give you an indication of how deep that conceptual understanding is:

Isolated	Connected
Recall	Justify
Describe	Explain

Technical proficiency.

Constructing a tool is all well and good. But it's useless unless it's used. Developing technical proficiency in the *use* of mental tools is just as important.

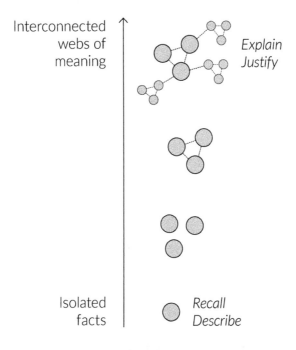

Interconnected
webs of
meaning

Explain
Justify

Isolated
facts

Recall
Describe

Fig. 4   Conceptual connectedness

Imagine you are trying to use your understanding of the area of a circle. To begin with you just want to get a feel for how that tool works. Get familiar with its most basic utility.

You might answer five fairly similar questions on finding the area given a radius. This will lead to a narrow yet proficient grasp of the basics of that tool.

You might then begin to tackle more complex and diverse problems, each a little more challenging than the last. Over time, this will lead to more adaptive proficiency.

Rigid	Adaptive
Follow	Solve
Find	Create

Knowledge ping pong.

The more you use a tool the more familiar you get with it. Developing technical proficiency can often lead to deeper conceptual understanding.

However, at some point you'll begin to sense the limits of the tool you are using, and want to return to the workshop for an upgrade.

This might involve adding to it, or swapping it for a more sophisticated model. But it can also involve taking your tool apart to help you better understand how it works.

Upgrading your tools makes them more powerful. Using your tools makes them more understandable. This iterative process is a core activity in the process of developing expertise.

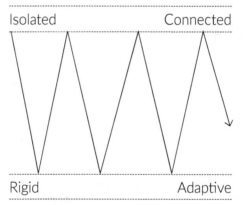

Increasing conceptual understanding

Isolated   Connected

Rigid   Adaptive

Increasing technical proficiency

Fig. 5   Building effective learning
trajectories

Get into the habit of asking yourself questions such as: **Is this lesson about building tools, or learning to use them better? What is the best order and interplay between these activities?**

Your answers to these questions will sharpen up your learning milestones, and give you a really clear sense of where you're headed in the lesson.

The clearer you are about **what** you want your pupils to learn, the better you will be able to help them get there.

Notes & further reading

1. Read about the TIMSS in *The Teaching Gap*
2. If anyone has come across any similar ideas, please let me know
3. Sometimes referred to as declarative and procedural knowledge
4. This model draws heavily on the *SOLO taxonomy* developed by Biggs & Collis

6

Checking understanding

When I reflect back over the hundreds of lesson observations I've done, one area for development comes up more than any other: the need to improve checking of understanding.

This is about **getting inside pupils' heads**. About generating *reliable* data to inform your action, by getting as deep into as many heads as possible, as quickly as possible. Because without this, you have a limited basis for making effective decisions about your teaching.

Improve how you check understanding and you will immediately increase your capacity for impact.

Let's look at the efficiency of some strategies[1.]

- **Single-student questioning** While posing questions to individual pupils can give you deep insights, it is a slow way to build up a picture of the understanding of the class.

- **Traffic-lighting** (or variants like thumbs up/down) Asking the class to indicate how confident they are can be useful in assessing and building meta-cognitive awareness, but it can be unreliable for assessing understanding[2].

- **Multi-student questioning** Posing a simple question that allows you to see everyone's answer can yield reliable data to inform your teaching. Examples include: using mini-whiteboards to show answers, or asking students to respond to multi-choice questions by holding up a particular hand signal.

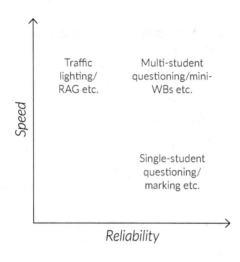

Fig. 6 Whole class assessment strategies

- **Diagnostic questioning** This variant of the above approach not only allows you to see who's getting it, but the misconceptions of those who aren't. For example: using mini-whiteboards to show reasoning, or framing your multi-choice questions so that incorrect answers highlight common misconceptions or mistakes[3].

The point here is not to get everyone using diagnostic questioning all the time, but to encourage you to consider *efficiency* when you plan your approach to assessment.

Greater efficiency allows you to generate more data, and so base decisions during planning and teaching on a more accurate picture of what students know and don't know.

> *"Perhaps the most salient characteristic of a great teacher is her ability to recognise the difference between I* taught *it and they* learned *it."*
> - Doug Lemov[4]

Exit assessment.

Effective diagnosis is not just a product of *how* you check understanding, but also *when* you do it. The best teachers employ high efficiency assessments at critical points during the lesson.

The end of your lesson is one of the more obvious times to check understanding. However, it is not always done well. Teachers can find themselves prone to the following:

1. **Overrunning** The environment of the classroom makes it easy to lose track of time and find yourself with no time left for exit assessment.
2. **Opting out** The energy demands of a lesson mean that sometimes it's just *easier* to let students continue with their current task rather than stop them for an exit assessment.

Both approaches limit future learning. Not creating the space for exit assessment will limit how well you can evaluate your teaching, and constrain your ability to plan effectively for future lessons.

Set a timer to go off X minutes before the end of the lesson, and use a **time boxed exit ticket**.

This is a small slip of paper with 3-5 questions that students complete within a certain time, and then hand to you as they walk out the door. The questions on this ticket have a dual purpose:

1. **Progress** To assess where students are on the path through the learning milestones.
2. **Prep** To establish aspects of prior knowledge to help you plan for a future lesson.

Transition assessment.

As well as assessing at exit, great teachers routinely check understanding in the transitions between activities in a lesson. For example, when moving from an explanation to a student-led activity.

Conducting a high efficiency understanding check at this point will quickly show you how many students have 'got' your explanation. If it's a majority, you can move on to your activity. If it's not, you may need to take a step back and help them **get** the parts they haven't got yet.

It's an opportunity to re-calibrate your teaching towards the needs of your students, to adapt your lesson to cater for what's unfolding around you, rather than blindly following a pre-determined path.

It's about basing your teaching on what your students know and don't know. It's about making informed decisions about when to 'move on'.

Entry Assessment.

Some teachers plan to assess prior knowledge at the beginning of a lesson. However, I'm not convinced this is useful, as it's too late to make any major changes to your teaching as a result.

Exit assessment is better suited to this goal. This also frees up the start of your lesson to help your students reconnect with relevant prior knowledge, an important strategy for building lasting learning.

More of this in Chapter 8, but first, we need to look at efficiency some more. This time, in the context of activity selection and design.

Notes & further reading

1. For more, read *Embedded Formative Assessment* by Dylan Wiliam
2. For more, see 'Reject self-report' in *Teach Like a Champion* 2.0 by Doug Lemov
3. Check out diagnosticquestions.com
4. In *Teach Like a Champion* 2.0, p.24

7

Efficient activities

"I have 4 [lessons to plan], and zero patience for the sort of purposeless googling that my planning used to involve."
- Michael Pershan[1]

Have you ever planned an activity that was more complex than it needed to be? Perhaps you were trying to inject some creativity, movement or collaboration into the lesson. Either way, it just didn't work out, despite all your preparation.

When it comes to planning for learning, less is often better.

Lean lesson planning is about reducing the noise and amplifying the signal, about focusing your attention on what is important and stripping away the clutter.

Because if it's not adding value, it's subtracting it.

> **NOTE** *When I talk about activities, I am referring to things like teacher explanation, modeling and questioning as well as more student-led tasks.*

Lemov's 'shortest path'.

Occam's law suggests that the simplest or most obvious solution is often the best. When crafting lean activities, ask yourself: **What is the least that needs to happen for my students to make progress towards their next learning milestone[2]?**

The idea here is not about taking shortcuts or dumbing down learning. And it's certainly not about eliminating things like creativity, movement or collaboration.

It's about selecting, streamlining and where necessary, *eliminating* activities so your students can approach their learning milestones as directly as possible. It's about what Lemov calls 'taking the shortest path'[3].

Teaching for attention.

Our classrooms are a microcosm of today's attention economy. Effective teachers treat student attention as a scarce commodity and consider the following.

- Constrain teacher-led talk to bursts of 5-10 minutes.
- Keep most activities to around 15 minutes, being sensitive to the costs of task-switching.
- Avoid tasks that require their students to focus on multiple things at once[4].

- Use activity structure instead of instruction where possible[5].

Ask yourself questions such as: **What is the least amount of explanation my students need before they can move on? What is the least amount of deliberate practice they need to make progress?**

Fun as a by-product.

When I talk about lean activities some teachers get concerned that they lack sufficient 'fun'. And that their students will become uninterested and stop learning as a result.

However, in my experience, success breeds the most enjoyment. Focus on helping your students *succeed* and they will not only have great fun, but will develop better attitudes towards their learning too[6]. Fun is important, but it is best treated as a by-product.

Success through challenge.

The aim of any lean activity is to help as many students as possible to feel success. Success happens where there is just enough challenge, but not too much.

Your goal is to keep as many students as you can in the zone of challenge, and out of the zones of comfort or confusion for as long as possible[7].

Here are a couple of activity types that can achieve this without excessive preparation:

- **Low floor, high ceiling** One task that is accessible to all, but can be taken as far as each student is able. These are often open-ended, or investigational in nature.
- **All start, no finish** A series of questions graduated in difficulty so everyone can answer the first one, but no one can answer the last.

It's also important to be ready to adjust the level of challenge as needed *during* an activity. One easy way to do this is by adding or removing supports, such as hint cards, writing frameworks or calculators.

One strategy that you should use with care is that of *letting your students move on early*, answering the next page in the textbook (or equivalent). This can sometimes create more problems than it solves. Aim to extend deeper rather than faster.

Feedback baked in.

Of all the factors that can leverage impact, feedback is possibly the most powerful. In John Hattie's analysis, it has almost twice the effect of the average of all the other effects[8].

Lean activities bake in opportunities for feedback as standard[9].

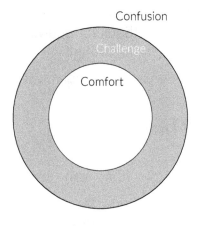

Fig. 7   Zones of learning (or not)

This does not always need to be teacher-led. Well-structured peer feedback and self-assessment can be powerful too. Feedback is effective when it[10]:

- Closes the gap between where students are and the next learning milestone.
- Focuses on how to help students move on, not on what went wrong.
- Is provided alongside multiple opportunities to put it into practice.
- Focuses on the single smallest thing that will help them make the most progress.
- Offers formative comments rather than marks.

Notes & further reading

5. From *How I plan: the triage* goo.gl/3E6bP1
6. For more, see Chapter 8: Minimum Viable Lessons in *The Thinking Teacher* by Oliver Quinlan
7. See *Teach Like a Champion* 2.0 by Doug Lemov, p.147
8. From *Visible Learning and the Science of How we Learn* by John Hattie, p.48
9. For more, read *Fewer instructions, better structures* by Ewan McIntosh goo.gl/AdqOV
10. From *Visible Learning and the Science of How we Learn* by John Hattie, p.39
11. Based on Lev Vygotsky's *Zone of Proximal Development*
12. From *Visible Learning for Teachers* by John Hattie, p.130
13. For inspiration on how to put this into practice, see *Moving from marking to feedback* by Harry Fletcher-Wood goo.gl/y421mn
14. For a comprehensive overview, read *Embedding Formative Assessment* by Dylan William

8

Lasting learning

One of the biggest challenges we face as teachers is helping students remember. Not just for the time it takes to complete a task, but long enough to be useful in an exam situation, and their lives beyond.

Lean lesson planning is about building lasting learning, not just lesson learning.

Lasting learning has happened if something can be recalled and used with ease several weeks after it was last formally explored during a lesson. It is a product of both **longevity and fluency**.

To create lasting learning, we need to build our planning around *how memory works*[1]. This is a fairly obvious idea, but not immediately obvious how to put it into practice.

Thinking less but better.

> *"Memory is the residue of thought."*
> - Daniel Willingham[2]

Learning happens when we think. The problem is that our brains have limited *bandwidth* for thinking (sometimes referred to as working memory or cognitive load). We can only think about so many things at any one time.

Fig. 8   Multi-tasking trade-off curve

The more things you try to think about in any one time, the poorer the quality of thought overall. Low quality thinking leaves less residue, and reduces the chances of making learning last.

"Multi-tasking
is the wrong option anytime you expect to learn,
acquire knowledge, or think deeply."
- John Hattie[3]

Not only is our brain limited by the number of things we can usefully think about at once, but it also suffers a delay every time we switch between tasks.

What is often referred to as multi-tasking is actually more like task-switching[4]. Eliminate unnecessary switching and you'll waste less thinking time in the long run.

When it comes to thinking, aim for doing less but doing it better.

The next time you plan a lesson or activity, ask yourself: **What exactly do I want my students to be thinking about? And what do I NOT want my students to be wasting their bandwidth on?**

Anchoring thinking.

> *"The most important single factor influencing learning is what the learner already knows."*
> - David Ausubel[3]

Learning lasts longer when students are able to build upon what they already know. Our brains are 'sense making' machines, and things that don't 'mean' anything to us (things that can't be linked to our existing frameworks of understanding) are quickly jettisoned[5.] *Anchor* new thinking by:

- Exploring what your students already know about the topic, and using this as a starting point when designing and selecting activities.

- Finding out what they are interested in and using this to create a context that is meaningful to them.
- Helping them identify connections between what they are learning and what they already know.

Concept mapping can be a powerful tool in helping to achieve these outcomes.

Spaced learning.

Memories have a half-life. Like a radioactive isotope, they gradually decay over time. Some memories have a short half-life, others longer. Their rate of decay depends on the conditions in which those memories were forged.

There are things we can do to make learning last longer.

Most new knowledge learnt at school starts with a short half-life. Leave it untouched and it will evaporate quickly. Revisit it before it disappears and you extend its life even longer.

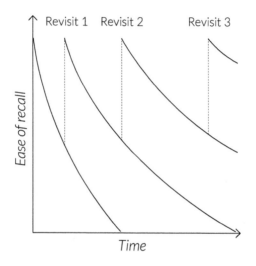

Fig. 9   Memory atrophy curve[6]

Every time you revisit a memory, you extend its half-life. Get the timing right, and you can build learning that lasts a long time.

You'll need to figure out the best rhythm for your situation, but here's a basic timeline for spaced learning (sometimes called distributed learning) to get you started:

1. **First encounter** Expose your students to an idea or process for the first time during part of a lesson.
2. **Days later** Reactivate that learning next time you see them, with a recap of key ideas, and a few consolidation activities.
3. **Weeks later** Repeat in a similar way a few lessons down the line, and again a few weeks later.

Between visits, it's important to alter the learning experience a little, but not too much. Add elements or change the context, but make sure the previous encounter is still highly recognizable[7.]

And don't forget to start from where they're at. Ask them: **What do you remember from the last time we explored this[8]?**

Deliberate practice.

> *"It's not* practise makes perfect, *it's* practise makes permanent."
> - Doug Lemov

To help your students recall with *fluency*, plan regular opportunities for **deliberate practice**. Experiment with the following approaches[9]:

- **Practice the core** Practice fewer, more important things in greater depth.
- **Practice first** Provide opportunities to consolidate existing understanding before being exposed to more.
- **Feed forward** Offer high quality feedback on how to improve alongside opportunities for further practice.
- **Graduated challenge** Increase the challenge little by little rather than in big jumps.

- **Bright spots** Practice things you are already good at, as well as what you need to improve.
- **Drill the basics** Drill basic ideas and processes to free up bandwidth for more complex learning.
- **Practice success** Practice learning from mistakes rather than making them.

The economics of practice.

Spaced learning and deliberate practice take time. Often, our first response as teachers to these ideas is: **I'd love to do more of this, but I have so much to cover that I just don't have the time.**

However, I'm not convinced this argument is economically sound. Not planning for memory will cost you more time in the long run. Your pupils will just end up revisiting topics again and again, struggling to develop longevity or fluency.

Furthermore, the issue compounds as students progress through school. Poor fluency in lower level topics can hinder their ability to learn higher level concepts and processes.

By contrast, fluency in the basics will allow your students to devote a greater proportion of their limited bandwidth to making progress with the harder stuff.

We're almost at the end of ACT II. We've explored various habits to improve your planning. But we need one more to pull it all together.

Notes & further reading

1. For a great introduction to this topic, see *Does memorisation get in the way of learning?* by Kris Boulton goo.gl/ekXtkn
2. *Why students don't like school?* by Daniel Willingham
3. See *Visible Learning and the Science of How we Learn* by John Hattie, p.187
4. In *Educational Psychology* by David Ausubel
5. *Visible Learning and the Science of How we Learn* by John Hattie, p.114
6. Based on the Ebbinghaus Forgetting curve
7. For a useful overview, see *The Hidden Lives of Learners* by Graham Nuthall
8. Stephen Lockyer uses what he calls *the 10:10:10 rule*: 10 second student summaries, repeated 10 minutes later, and once again 10 days later
9. Drawing heavily on ideas from *Practice Perfect* by Doug Lemov, and *An Ethic of Excellence* by Ron Berger

9

Inter-lesson planning

"Expert teachers plan lessons as interlinked sequences."
- John Hattie[1]

By now, you'll have realized that lean lesson planning extends beyond individual lessons. It treats learning as a thinking experience that happens over time, not something that can be divided up neatly into lesson-sized portions.

The relationship *between* lessons is just as important as what happens within them.

Restorative planning.

In the previous chapter, we discussed how learning happens when memories become permanent, not just when they first get a foothold. This has implications for the idea of **Backwards planning** that we explored in Chapter 4.

It is no longer enough just to ask yourself: What do I want my students to have learnt by the end of the lesson?

We've also got to ask: **What previous learning do we need to revisit in today's lesson?**

To answer the second question, we want to think back to the previous lesson, and the one from last week, and possibly even one from last month.

Lean lesson planning is an exercise in restoring learning. It's as much about making your teaching timely, as it is about making it efficient.

'Back to the future' planning.

When you sit down to plan a lesson, as well as thinking back to previous learning, you'll want to think forward to future learning. Get into the habit of asking yourself: **What prior knowledge do I need to assess today so I can plan properly for my next lesson?**

At this stage you might be thinking: this sounds like hard work. And it will be to begin with. But as it begins to develop into a habit, you'll find it becomes an easy and natural part of your planning. And at some point, it'll become hard *not* to do it.

We're now entering the territory of disciplined professional improvement, of innovation, collaboration and habit architecture. Strap in. It's time for ACT III.

Notes & further reading

1. *Visible Learning and the Science of How we Learn* by John Hattie, p.104

ACT III

Habits for growing

10

Building excellence

"We are what we repeatedly do. Excellence, then, is not an act, but a habit."
- Aristotle

We are creatures of habit. Many of the decisions we make and actions we take on any typical day are the result of our habits and routines.

Our approach to planning is no exception. It's just another routine we have developed over time. A stack of habits of thought.

Relying on habit is not necessarily a bad thing. Habits allow us to achieve lots and achieve it quickly, with minimal effort. They allow us to focus our attention on the things that matter.

Habits only pose a risk if we become unaware of them, and they fall out of alignment with our goals.

Unfortunately, it's all too easy for this to happen, resulting in poorer performance and feelings of frustration.

You can read about the tactics explored in ACT II of this book as often as you like, but little will change unless you have a clear plan for integrating them into your daily routine.

Lean lesson planning is not just an approach to optimizing your impact in the classroom. It is an exercise in disciplined self-improvement.

Let's explore some strategies you can use to change your habits.

Mindful awareness.

Mindfulness is about becoming more aware of what you are doing, and more deliberate about what you want to do.

This includes your thoughts and feelings, as well as your actions.

One of the best ways to sharpen your mindfulness is to devote a bit of time each day to practicing it in a controlled environment. The skills you develop here will then spill over into other parts of your day.

There are plenty of resources available to help get you up and running[1].

The more you practice mindfulness, the more you'll begin to notice your habits of behavior and thought.

As an experiment, try setting an alarm to go off at random times during the day, pause and ask yourself: **What exactly am I doing now? Is it what I would *choose* to do?**

Habit architecture.

The more you become aware of your habits and routines, the more you'll want to improve them. For this to work, the changes you make need to satisfy two criteria.

1. They need to align more closely with your goals
2. They need to last

Changing the way you behave and think is no easy task. Here are some steps you can take to increase your chances of making it happen:

1. **Identify** Get a clear picture of how you currently plan. Write down what you think and do from start to finish.

2. **Ideate** Decide what your ideal planning routine would look like. Think about all you've learned in this book, and map it out.
3. **Isolate** Choose one tiny thing you can change about your current planning routine that will take you closer to your ideal routine.
4. **Inspect** Create a checklist to remind you of that one tiny thing, stick it somewhere you will see, and track how your change is holding out.
5. **Iterate** Once that tiny change starts to feel natural and easy to maintain, it's time to make another. Add that to your checklist. Rinse and repeat.

This process is deliberately slow. Unless you are a new teacher, your planning routines will have built up a fair bit of inertia. Lasting change demands both patience and persistence.

Environmental optimization.

Just like putting chocolate on the top shelf of your cupboard can be a powerful tactic in the battle against sugar snacks[2], modifying the environment in which you plan can ultimately influence the quality of your teaching[3.]

Think about *where* and *when* you plan, and ask yourself: **What changes could I make to my setup that would improve my planning?**

Often this boils down to finding a time and place where there will be no interruptions or distractions. Close the door and put your phone away. The complex and creative demands of planning deserve your undivided attention.

First stepping.

The first step in any journey is the one that is most prone to failure. Get off the blocks and you will have infinitely increased your chances of making subsequent progress[4].

If you're interested in improving your planning and increasing your impact in the classroom, take that first step with me right now.

It doesn't have to be big. In fact, the smaller the better. At the end of this page, put down this book and take one tiny action to represent your first step on the journey towards lean lesson planning.

And don't come back till you're done.

> *"The journey of a thousand miles begins with one step."*
> *- Lao Tzu*

Welcome to the lean lesson planning club.

Robo-teacher?

> *"Automacy works in synergy with deep thinking."*
> - John Hattie

Just before we end this chapter, I want to reassure you that I'm not trying to turn you into a lifeless automaton.

Imagination flourishes in environments of change and constraint. Habit realignment will make you *more* creative and excited about your planning and teaching, not less.

And with regards to the slow, incremental nature of change, get comfortable with it, because it can be addictive.

Once you get going, your ideal planning routine will continue to evolve. Your checklist will become a touchstone for your growth.

Habit architecture will become a habit in itself.

This chapter has outlined how you might improve. The next explores how we can do it in the right direction.

> "On your journey towards your goal, at some point you will realise that you have changed into someone who is good at getting places. You may never get to your original goal, but you will be better nonetheless."
> - Norman Peale

Notes & further reading

1. The Headspace app is a great place to start
2. Hi, my name is Peps and I have a chocolate problem.
3. For more, read *Switch* by Chip and Dan Heath
4. For more, see tinyhabits.com

11

Growth teaching

"It is well documented that people can spend years performing activities without actually increasing their expertise."
- John Hattie[1]

The study explored in Chapter 5 also compared the different ways that various countries sought to improve their education systems.

During the 30-year period studied, the U.S. tried to implement several big, radical changes, whereas Japan spent their time building a culture of gradual, incremental improvement. Japan's approach achieved better results.

Lean lesson planners adopt a similar strategy. They focus on making small, everyday changes to their teaching, and strive to understand the impact of those changes.

The goal of the lean lesson planner is not *great* teaching, but *growth* teaching. Teaching that is constantly getting better. Better than yesterday, better than last year, and some day, better than great.

It's about the aggregation of marginal gains. And avoiding the plateau[2].

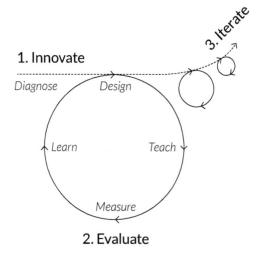

Fig. 10   Growth teaching curve

Here's a simple framework you can use to power growth teaching.

- **Diagnose** Identify a part of your teaching to improve
- **Design** Develop a (potentially) better approach
- **Teach** Try it out in your classroom over time
- **Measure** Evaluate the impact of this new approach
- **Learn** Figure out what's happening. Rinse and repeat

Growth teachers are forever tinkering with their practice, and striving to understand the impact of those changes.

They spend a lot of time engaged in innovation and evaluation, with the goal of continually iterating their impact. Here are some things to consider along the way.

Evidence-informed teaching?

At the **Design** stage you'll often want to look to relevant research for inspiration. Sometimes there'll be evidence to guide you, sometimes there won't. Sometimes you'll choose to use it, other times you won't.

This is all good. Building practice around evidence about what works can be a powerful strategy in improving your practice, but it's only part of the longer-term solution.

Most educational research currently exists downstream of innovation, and so it can only ever inform you of what's been tried and tested. Sometimes you'll need to step upstream, and innovate from first principles.

If you *are* using evidence, then it's best to treat it as a starting point for **experimentation in context**, rather than an off-the-shelf technique that you can plug and play.

Impact evaluation.

*"Passion for evaluating impact is the single most
critical lever for instructional excellence."*
- John Hattie[3]

After you've designed and trialed a new approach,
you'll want to evaluate it.

Don't try to evaluate too soon. Give your approach
a chance to fully unfold. Often you'll have to
overcome the inertia of familiarity, and the novelty
of the new, before you can start to see the lasting
potential of a change.

Besides, there is little value in exploring new
teaching strategies until you've got a firm feel for
the impact of existing ones.

Ask yourself: **What impact is this approach having
on learning? How does it *work*?**

Balanced evaluation.

The most robust evaluation combines multiple approaches[4.]

1. **Progress indicators** Data from your exit-tickets, in-class assessments and results from scheduled tests.
2. **Observational perspectives** Feedback from any adults in the room, or any self-video recordings you've set up.
3. **Student surveys** Feedback from students using targeted questions, via post-it notes, exit-tickets or good old *face-to-face* at the end of the lesson.

This *trio of indicators* will generate data to help inform your evaluation. Evaluation without data is just reflection.

Your aim here is not only to assess the impact of new practices, but also to figure out **how** they are working. Ask yourself: **How does this change make things different?**

Impact iteration is as much about understanding your teaching as making it better.

Common challenges.

The complexity of learning and your position in the classroom make evaluation a challenging task.

We're generally not great at unpicking our own practice, but that doesn't mean we shouldn't be doing it.

We just need to take extra care to avoid some common tendencies.

- **Cognitive biases** In particular situations we tend to make bad judgments using poor logic[5].
- **Premature conclusions** We have a desire to make bold statements, and jump to early conclusions.
- **Proxy indicators** We often give visible indicators of learning (eg. engagement, busyness) too much weight in evaluating learning (which is invisible)[6].

The whole process may seem like a lot of work. And to begin with it is. But over time it will start to feel like a natural part of your practice. And eventually, you will feel naked without it.

Besides, it's worth the effort. Do you really want to go to work each day not really understanding what you're doing or how it could be better?

Growth teaching is great to do on your own, but it is even more effective when done with others. The next (and final) chapter explores how we might *get better together.*

Notes & further reading

1. *Visible Learning and the Science of How we Learn* by John Hattie, p.40
2. For more, watch David Weston's TEDtalk *How do we develop great teaching?*
3. *Visible Learning for Teachers* by John Hattie, p.viii
4. *Designing Teacher Evaluation Systems* by Kane et al.
5. For a strong overview, read *What if everything you knew about education was wrong?* by David Didau, cp.2
6. For more, see *Engagement: just because they're busy doesn't mean they're learning* by Carl Hendrick goo.gl/cM2f96

12

Collective improvement

"The co-planning of lessons is the task that has one of the highest likelihoods of making a marked positive difference on student learning."
- John Hattie[1]

For a profession organized around learning, I am always surprised at how little time we spend actually talking about teaching. About what we do in the classroom and why. Hattie suggests that in some contexts, this happens for as little as one minute per month[2].

And yet, sharing practice is a powerful lever for improvement. If we want things to get better, we need to make collaboration a routine activity.

Sharing practice makes you articulate what you are doing and why. It creates space for reflection, brings fresh eyes to old problems, and spreads our understanding of what works (and what doesn't) amongst the profession.

Sharing practice simply makes sense.

> "The star teachers of the twenty-first century will be teachers who work every day to improve teaching - not only their own but that of the whole profession."
> - Stigler & Hiebert[3]

Lean lesson planners see sharing as a core part of their job.

The next time you find yourself with another teacher, ask them: **What are you working on in your classroom? What are you learning about?**

The likelihood is you'll have a *great* conversation.

Creating space to share.

One of the reasons I suspect teachers talk so little about their practice is because the job is just so intense. In those few small breaks you *do* get during a day, it's healthy to talk about other things.

So when is a good time? School leaders could do a lot worse than to provide their staff with an hour every week or two, a protected agenda, and some tea and biscuits to ease the sharing.

Beyond school, Teachmeets, Teachcamps, and training days can be powerful experiences. They provide space and time to talk and think with colleagues outside your immediate context.

There's also the option of digital sharing. Tools like Twitter, Wordpress and Staffrm[4] allow us to build professional learning networks around our values and interests.

Crucially, these tools allow us to do things in our own space and time, and so build collaborative routines around our lives, in flexible and sustainable ways.

Structuring sharing.

How you share your learning and practice can influence how useful and memorable it is for others. Increase your chances of having an impact by using a framework to package your pedagogy[5].

1. **Isolate** What am I currently focusing on and why?
2. **Situate** What context am I doing this in?
3. **Validate** How do I know when it's working (or not)?
4. **Narrate** How did this come about and what's next?
5. **Kickstart** How can someone else get started with this?

Teachers spend so much time thinking. They make great progress during their careers. Yet so much of this knowledge leaves with them when they move on from the profession.

Imagine a school where every teacher shared what he or she were working on and learning about.

And then imagine a whole world where every teacher did the same.

Now go make it happen.

> *"If we can find a way to marshal the efforts &*
> *experiences of our millions of teachers the potential*
> *is far greater than anything that can be achieved by a*
> *few thousand researchers."*
> - Stigler & Hiebert[6]

Notes & further reading

1. *Visible Learning for Teachers* by John Hattie, p.viii
2. From *The Educators* podcast goo.gl/2HOljB
3. *The Teaching Gap* by Stigler & Hiebert, p.179
4. *Disclosure:* I am a founder of Staffrm
5. Inspired by various *pedagogical pattern frameworks*
6. *The Teaching Gap* by Stigler & Hiebert, p.136

Metalogue

I'm deeply passionate about helping teachers get better. If you have suggestions for how this book could be improved, please do get in touch, I'd love to hear from you.

And if this book has helped you, spread the word. Tell your colleagues, write a blog-post, and if you're feeling extra-generous, leave a quick one-line review on Amazon.

Happy planning.

Peps
pepsmccrea@gmail.com
twitter/@pepsmccrea

Thank you

Carol & Richard for the opportunity.

Jeremy for introducing me to this world.

Lockyer for being a bad influence.

Em for not goading me too much.

And **Mum and Dad** for their limitless support.

MEMORABLE TEACHING

Peps Mccrea

EXPERT
TEACHING

Peps Mccrea

MOTIVATED TEACHING

Peps Mccrea

Notes

Notes

CPSIA information can be obtained
at www.ICGtesting.com
Printed in the USA
JSHW021355050123
35599JS00002B/4

9 781912 906680